Gérard Dalmaz **MONT-SAINT-MICHEL**

ÉDITIONS DU PATRIMOINE

CENTRE DES
MONUMENTS NATIONAUX

INTRODUCTION

A giant reliquary in a titanic baptistery

It is one of two things: either, once you have arrived on the shores of this bay that earth and sea fight over, 2 kilometres as the seagull flies from the silhouette of Mont-Saint-Michel— the mount, "cathedral's tiara and fortress's breastplate" (Victor Hugo)—the mystery of this "Kheops of the West" gets you right there, or you have the fleeting feeling of having already lived this moment, so much is the photo of the jewel in its eyrie setting imprinted on the retina of the world's memory. One way or another, the imagination races faced with the strangeness of the stone vessel and its forlorn rowing boat, Tombelaine, moored forever in the silvery mirror of France's largest bay.

An enormous masterpiece of horizontal vertigo, with fatal dangers. The granite of the sanctuary defies the invading sand, especially since the small coastal rivers were tamed. What's more, the sediment accumulates around the causeway. Since 1879 the maritime mount has been nothing more than a peninsula. Patience, the 21st century is putting right the sacrilege. Who were the madmen, the visitor wonders, who dared cling to this inaccessible place, to perch their City of God there, blessed twice a day by the English Channel in its titanic baptistery, even though the surrounding countryside is more hospitable?

Then up looms a surreal satellite two cables' length from its mainland origins, a giant reliquary in proud solitude, like an image from a science-fiction comic.

On this abruptly mineral world, the servants of our Heavenly Father put up their citadel of the faith dedicated to the prince of the celestial armies, the archangel Saint Michael: the knight of good versus evil, who defeated the dragon, Satan, the prince of demons.

The mount in the summer morning mist. Right, the profile of the rock Tombelaine stands out against the bank of the River Cotentin.

3

What more natural then, for beings hungry for spiritual retreat (monk, from the Greek *monos*, "alone"), than to choose this place well away from the unrest, foolishness, and temptations of the brutal world? By its very nature, this incredibly pyramid-like piece of confetti was sacred from the beginning. It could *only* exist through divine intervention. It was obviously a "sacred hill", one of the "chosen places from the beginning of time" (Maurice Barrès). It was thus marked out to praise the Most High and His pantheon, if that could be said about this Acropolis of Christianity.

Faith adorns the mountain

Hugo sums up the situation: "Mont-Saint-Michel, the work of nature and of man."
Faith only moved the mountain. Here, it adorns the peak (80 metres) with architectural feats and decorative refinements: for the glory and pleasure of God first, then for the renown of the monks, and, finally, to attract the maximum number of pilgrims.
Thirteen hundred years of construction, collapses, catastrophes, storms, modifications, fires (twelve), plundering, strokes of genius, and questionable interventions (prison, workshops, restorations): all this could have ended up in a jumble of additions. This was clearly not the case: harmony emerges from the multiple layers of constructions, a maze. Gustave Flaubert would say: "One gets lost in it. A single visit is not enough to understand the complicated plan." The dozens of abbots managed to match that which came before and not to hinder what might follow. The whole and its halo of mysticism would make a suitable setting for a Gothic detective story like *The Name of the Rose*.
Still commercial, still kneeling at the foot of the abbey and huddled against the ramparts, mostly dating from the Hundred Years War, the village has barely changed since the Middle Ages and the flood of pilgrims. Hence its charm and industriousness. Up high, around the abbey church's flamboyant choir, on the crown of flying buttresses, the pinnacles stretch out their stone fingers as if to beseech the protection of the archangel that tops the spire at over 157 metres, wings in the sky or head in the clouds of the changeable Normandy sky.

On this setting, in various shades of grey, is the patina of the centuries: golden lichens and biting sea spray on the boulders hewn from the Chausey Islands. No fear, the thick granite withstands the north-west and north winds, permanent guests. This treasure of humanity, along with the bay's ecosystem, the village, and the fortifications, has been on the World Heritage List since 1979 and was the first French site to figure on this list. This combination of beauty, enigmas, achievements, medieval romance, and souvenirs explains why Mont-Saint-Michel is France's third most visited site, after the Eiffel Tower and the Château de Versailles: 3.5 million visitors, mostly foreign, a third of whom make the trip to the abbey. For a thousand years, pilgrims came in their tens of thousands to the Heavenly Jerusalem. Now, millions of tourists from all over the world come to see the timeless hill.

After the Porte de l'Avancée, the entrance to the village (fortified in 1525). In the foreground: the Porte du Boulevard. In the background: the Porte du Roi (1435). The Mère Poulard, which may be seen to the left, was built nearby in 1888. Around 1985 the architect Pierre-André Lablaude restored the Porte du Roi to its original state: drawbridge, portcullis, moat, and door leaves reinforced with iron plates (photograph by Neurdein, Henry Decaëns collection).

MI-KA-ËL, "Who is like God?"

The mount's first miracle was its existence, which dates back to the dawn of time, 540 million years ago, when erosion began to smooth away the schist of the Hercynian folding. A few granite outcrops resisted and are still present: the sentinel of Mont-Saint-Michel, its handmaiden Tombelaine, and their comrade Mont-Dol, now in the seaside marshes. Above it, the thaw of the last glaciation raised the level of the seas. In the thousands of years before year zero, the mount became an island. The bay's vegetation was eliminated by the saltwater (fossilised trunks). The bay was not yet clogged and navigation remained possible for a long period.

The mound, unusual in the endless flatness, was then occupied by the pagan rites of solar divinities inherited from the Celts, Gauls, Romans, and the Middle East, such as Ogmios, Taranis, Cybele, Belenus, Lugus, Apollo, and Mercury, or the Persian Mithra honoured at the nearby Mont-Dol. No evidence relating to the mount has survived.

As for the archangel, God's first lieutenant shone in the Eastern firmament of Christian forms of worship (Copts). He made himself indispensable in the Book of Revelation (New Testament) by casting out the Dragon, "which deceiveth the whole world". Lucifer set himself up as a rival to God. God's constable, who was not yet called Michael, scathingly asked him, "Who is like God?"—MI-KA-ËL (in Hebrew)—who dares claim to be God's equal? This question became the name of the victor.

In the late 5th century, the cult of Saint Michael began in southern Italy, on Monte Gargano, where the archangel appeared in a cave that was immediately turned into a sanctuary.

There was a dramatic turn of events in Avranches in 708: Bishop Aubert, according to the *Revelatio*, a legend written 150 years later, was visited by Saint Michael in a dream. The prelate was sceptical, wary of the trickery of Mephistopheles. The impatient archangel pointed a finger at him: "Get this in your head, I need *my own* sanctuary!" Aubert obeyed, sending clerics to the summit of the bay's alluvial cone to build a grotto like that of Monte Gargano. According to the *Revelatio*, a certain Bain and his twelve sons cleared an enormous boulder from the land that some thought was the menhir of a contemptible idol.

God's walkers on their paths to heaven

In 966 the Vikings were "Normanised". They no longer terrorised the Avranches region. The clerics of Mont-Saint-Michel became wealthy canons. The duke of Normandy turned them out in favour of twelve monks, followers of Saint Benedict, a key figure now considered one of Europe's forefathers. Charlemagne, who is thought to have visited the mount, supported Benedictine Rule throughout the empire; he also imposed the cult and feast day of Saint Michael (29 September). The islet was then named Mont-Tombe, from *tumba* and/or tumulus: hillock and later grave, which results in a strange "mount-mount" (Tombelaine: small mount). Work on the abbey began in the 10th century and was not completed until the 16th century. The imitation grotto desired by Bishop Aubert, too cramped, was replaced by the chapel of Notre-Dame. Half Carolingian, half Romanesque, the chapel, then above ground, became the Crypte de Notre-Dame-sous-Terre, as it supported the church's entrance and square. At the back of the crypt, the oldest in the abbey, is a wall of bonded rough stones that we hope is the last surviving trace of the original grotto. The mount has not revealed all of its secrets. In this crypt remains the brickwork raised platform where relics used to be placed high up so that they could only be approached in order to prevent people from taking the holy relics, certified as being authentic.

The paths to heaven leading pilgrims to the Heavenly Jerusalem began their international career in the 9th century. The *miquelots* (pilgrims) were attracted by the virtues of the relics, reputed to cure certain illnesses—the pierced skull of Saint Aubert was thought to relieve persistent migraines—and above all to absolve sins. Saint Michael, in addition to his two-edged sword, lance, and shield, was equipped with scales to weigh souls during the Last Judgement. This role was undoubtedly inspired by ancient beliefs (Anubis). In the Middle Ages, the archangel Michael was the link between the world below and the kingdom of God. One thus had to go to "his place" to get to heaven. As there were more and more pilgrims, the rock and the village became a hive of activity. Prosperity grew thanks to donations, as well as to the generous gifts of the Norman lords keen to favour their mount, a strategic fief and flagship of Christendom.

The church is nothing without support

The year is 1064: on the Bayeux Tapestry, the future William the Conqueror, protector of the mount, rides on horseback by the side of his future adversary Harold. Both cross the swampy ground of the estuary of the Couesnon, in the bay. Above them, the mount's summit is symbolised by the narthex of the abbey church, which was being completed. The Romanesque monastery settled on the north face of the rock, the steepest. The abbots (from *abba*, "father" in Aramaic) would have preferred the standard Benedictine horizontal plan, but the lie of the land was not suitable. Moreover, the summit was reserved for the abbey church. From 1023 to 1084 the building was 80 metres long, but the granite of the summit was only 25 metres long. Only the transept crossing was built on the rock. The support of the crypts was thus needed. Under the choir, to the east, is the Crypte des Gros Piliers. Under the south transept is the Crypte de Saint-Martin and its daring vault with a span of 9 metres, symbol of the celestial vault, of eternal time. It is also the proof of the precise calculations of the loads and thrusts by the architects and stonecutters. Under the north transept, on the monastery side, the Crypte de Notre-Dame-des-Trente-Cierges is dedicated to the Virgin, whose importance was renewed in the 12th century with the development of the doctrine of purgatory. Around 1060 the Romanesque monks' ambulatory was built; around 1140, it was altered by the very first local use of Gothic architecture (intersecting ribs), a technique imported from the Île-de-France through the circulation of ideas and borrowed manuscripts. The 11th century saw the peaceful reign of William the Conqueror, a period beneficial for both work on the abbey and monastic life. Between 1050 and 1075, the monk copyists and illuminators of the scriptorium made the mount famous with their calligraphy and manuscripts with first decorated, then historiated initials. It was the golden age of the mount's style. The entire Western world would long be envious of the "City of Books".

Philippe Auguste comes to the mount's aid

In the late 11th and early 12th centuries, work on the church and monastery was no bed of roses. The abbey rebelled against the dukes of Normandy, while the monks split up into clans and cliques for or against the investiture of such-and-such an abbot. There was an increasing number of collapses, probably because of the lack of stability of buildings erected on the sugar-loaf slopes. To top it all off, there were many fires, especially those caused by lightning. And then (shock, horror!), the in-house Benedictines stooped to creature comforts—the monks lived on the income from their colossal estate.

The light at the end of the tunnel was the arrival for thirty-two years (1154–86) of a man of calibre at the head of the abbey: Robert de Torigni, who did not trifle with the Rule of Saint Benedict—or with his authority or prestige. He was the confidant of popes and kings, Louis VII and especially Henry II of England. The abbot set everything right, so much so that under him the abbey attained its material, land ownership, and financial peak. Torigni even had new buildings erected: his residence, two more towers for the church, and guest quarters for distinguished pilgrims. It was the monastery's real hour of glory, accentuated by its spiritual and intellectual aura. The abbot, with his taste for literature, had his copyists work ceaselessly and above all put together a very diverse library of religious and secular works, which readers from all over Europe came to consult. The reputation of the abbey's scriptorium, like those of other abbeys, was extinguished during the 13th century by the lay workshops of universities such as the Sorbonne in Paris. There, not far from the future Boulevard Saint-Michel, the abbey owned the Collège du Mont, where novices studied. Certain intellectual and urbane abbots, such as Pierre Le Roy or Robert Jolivet, "the traitor", appreciated this residence.

In 1204 Normandy was claimed by King John of England, but Philippe Auguste won it back by the sword. His Breton allies set fire to the mount. To be forgiven by his new subjects, the king bestowed generous gifts on them. This godsend, combined with the mount's prosperity (increase in the number of pilgrims), allowed for the construction in twenty years (1210–30) of the new Gothic monastery on the site of its Romanesque predecessor. An architectural feat immediately called the Merveille (the Marvel) because it filled the pilgrims who came to its feet from the north with wonder. "The Marvel of the West" would become the emblem of an eternal France.

Mount and marvel

Buildings wound around the mount, tirelessly intertwining. The mount's major success is its Merveille, a marriage of opposing forces. Imagine the astonishment of the pilgrims cautiously crossing the bay with its traps, from the north, via the island of Tombelaine. They would see a cliff armed with powerful buttresses. While approaching, they would raise their eyes to this marvel of verticality: 50 metres high and 80 metres long. A skyscraper for the period.

Work on the new monastery was thought to have been carried out briskly with cheek and faultless technical skill in order to entrench such a weight, such organisation of the rooms on the most difficult slope. A magnificent result with an interior to match the exterior. The building is made up of two blocks placed side by side. They both comprise three superimposed

Left-hand page

The initial P of "*postquam*". Saint Gregory the Great, *Dialogues, c.* 1060. An illustration from the time of William the Conqueror inscribed in a quadrilateral: the Earth. The loop of the P opens a window onto eternity. As for the descender of the P, Saint Irenaeus said that while God is circumference, He acts in a straight line (Avranches, Bibliothèque Municipale, ms. 101, fol. 77 verso).

Section of the Merveille's east building with three floors, corresponding to medieval social hierarchy. Bottom: the almonry for the *lavatores*. Above: the Salle des Hôtes for the *bellatores*. At the top: the refectory for the *oratores*. Drawing by Émile Sagot, pen and ink and watercolour, *c.* 1865 (Paris, MAP).

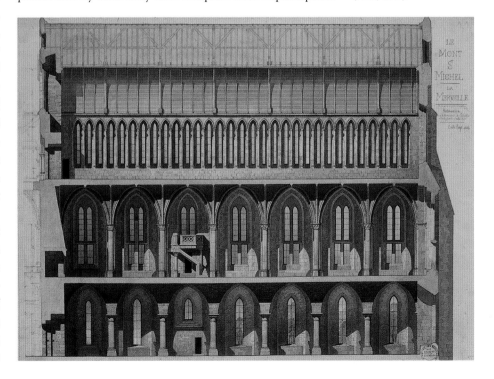

spaces, or six extraordinary rooms amongst the twenty-three rooms that can be visited in the abbey. On a vertical cutaway, the east building is made up of three dining rooms. Below was the almonry for the underlings; above, the Salle des Hôtes; and above that, at the top, the peerless refectory. Still vertical, in the west block, below: the storeroom; above, the room known as the Salle des Chevaliers; and above that the sublime cloister. This vertical ternary system corresponds to the religious and feudal conception of the social hierarchy of the time, and even of the entire *Ancien Régime* (the three orders of 1789). Three indissociable categories: at the bottom of the ladder were those who worked and produced; above were those who fought to protect the entire population; and above them were those who prayed to save everybody's souls. Evidently, the monks imposed their primacy over the other categories.

A procession of crowned heads

The almonry's lower hall is somewhat archaic as it reused the Romanesque remains that survived the fire of 1204. Its two seven-bay naves served as a soup kitchen for the countless pilgrims arriving in a sorry state. The food came from the adjoining ground-floor lower hall: the storeroom. It, too, was rustic, although Gothic. The supplies, including the provisions for sieges, were stored there using a dray ladder, a kind of steeple jack-crane, hauling up provisions and barrels from the small crafts moored at the foot of the marvellous wall.

In 1256 Louis IX made a pilgrimage (and returned in 1264). Saint Louis is said to have preferred to share the monks' meals in the refectory above, rather than feast in the Salle des Hôtes, a spectacular Gothic nave equipped with the latest conveniences: fireplaces and latrines. The Merveille was adorned with bright colours at the time, as was much of the abbey's decor.

Besides Saint Louis, responsible for the first real fortifications of the mount, the Salle des Hôtes would see several crowned heads blending gratitude, piety, and politics: Philippe III le Hardi (Philip the Bold, 1272); Philippe IV le Bel (Philip the Fair, 1311), donor of 1,200 gold ducats; Charles VI in 1393 and 1394—his insanity was not cured but the daughter born to him shortly after was named Michelle. Louis XI stayed at Mont-

Saint-Michel in 1462 before returning several times. The deeply religious king fell in love with the mount and its rather convenient remoteness. Louis XI chose one of the abbey's dungeons to hang one of his sinister cages, known as *fillettes*. The mount thus began its role as the "Bastille by the sea". François I visited twice (1518, 1532), the second time to meet the navigator Jacques Cartier (Canada). The last king to make a pilgrimage to the mount was Charles IX, who went in 1562 with his brother, the future Henri III, just before the Wars of Religion.

Next to the Salle des Hôtes is the room known as the Salle des Chevaliers. Apart from a board listing the names of the 119 knights who did not perish at the defeat at Agincourt (1415) and who took refuge on the mount to continue the combat against the English (free France against the occupying forces), there were no knights in this handsome, solidly built room, the largest in the Merveille. The name could come from the founding by Louis XI of the Order of Saint Michael in Amboise in 1469. Perhaps the abbey intended the room for the annual gathering of the thirty-six knights of the order, who never actually met there. The comfortable Salle des Chevaliers was probably used as a warming room, library, and scriptorium. It has two fireplaces, sparing the monk copyists and illuminators (eleven of whose names are known) from having hands numb with cold and from dipping their goose quills into frozen ink.

The marvels of the Merveille

On the floor above the Salle des Hôtes and the Salle des Chevaliers, at the top of the Merveille, was the exclusive domain of the agents of collective redemption: two stunningly innovative Gothic spaces, the cloister and the refectory. They are the brilliant demonstration of streamlining combined with design, and of the adaptation of the premises to Benedictine Rule. In the Merveille, there is stepping on three levels, while the monastery according to Saint Benedict should be built flat *around* the cloister, *the* spiritual centre of those praying for the salvation of society. This cloister is located at the summit, virtually ethereal or, in the words of the medievalist Georges Duby, "open to the movements of the sky and the reflections of the sea". It thus prefigures heaven even more accurately.

A rectangle of 25 metres by 14 metres, both austere and pleasant, its centre is adorned with a simple garden, undoubtedly to prevent it from inspiring daydreams.

On the perimeter, the gallery, covered by a wooden pointed barrel vault, is supported by a double row of 137 small columns of crimson pudding stone. The staggered layout, elegant and stable, was hailed by the young architect Eugène Viollet-le-Duc in 1835. This is where the monks read, meditated, and pondered the word of God and His staff captain.

Above the small columns, the greyish-beige limestone arches are decorated with sculpted spandrels, foliage in relief that used to be painted in bright colours: this botanical and floral diversity symbolises God's abundant creation. It is the evocation of the Garden of Eden and the perfect world to be rediscovered as man lived in harmony with God there. Despite the defacements of the Revolution and the vandalism of the 19th-century prisoners, a few figures, including that of Saint Francis of Assisi dating from 1228, can be made out. From the death of Il Poverello in 1226, the designers of the cloister wanted to sculpt a permanent homage to him.

Dragons—the Devil—are reminders that evil and temptation are everywhere and always threats. The organisation of the small columns is so ingenious that an optical illusion "rounds off" the four corners of the cloister. This animates the gallery with a sort of unchanging circular movement without beginning or end: perpetual.

Numbers to decipher

From top to bottom, all over the abbey, including the church, the famous music of numbers is evident if you pay attention to the numbers of the blind arcades, columns, windows, bays, and floors. Don't yield to the temptation of pseudo-esoteric wild imaginings: it is simply a question of mathematics, dogma, and theology.

A few examples: one is God; three, the Trinity, the Spirit; four, matter, Creation, the body, man; seven, the Earth plus the Spirit (137 small columns). The seven also signifies the Creation in six days becoming perfect with the addition of the one of God. Twelve (four times three) is plenitude, matter, and the Spirit, the Universal Church, the apostles. Nine is none other than renewal and the Virgin. An interesting detail: this music of numbers prefers the power of odd numbers, indivisible and thus pure and eternal.

Symbolic sacred geometry, this system of thought was inherited from the Neoplatonists and Pythagoras. It was nothing more than the taste for proportions. This harmony was also advocated by the Doctor of Grace, Saint Augustine, and put into practice by the savoir-faire of the Gothic new wave.

The Merveille's other gem: the refectory

The cloister, of Persian—the paradisiacal enclosed garden—then of Gallo-Roman descent, was at the centre of community life as it opened on to all the main spaces of the enclosure, including the adjoining refectory, undoubtedly the abbey's most beautiful room because of its sober elegance and perfect lighting. The master builder decided to illuminate a closed box with the light of God; the "Black Monks", as they were known, had to make do with natural light only. The anonymous genius used a hybrid—Romanesque for the volume and Gothic for the lines.

This lighting can be experienced as you move through the room. To the left and to the right, separated by small columns, the fifty-nine windows "open" in turn and "close" nearly immediately, with your footsteps. A marvel of subdued lighting, practically that of a painter's studio.

The monks' meals on the mount were not frugal because their days were long and hard, interspersed with prayers, in a harsh climate. They could not eat the meat of four-footed animals, but there were cakes and wine. Speech was proscribed by the rule of silence (which also applied in the cloister, dormitory, and church). To communicate with one's neighbour—for example, "Please past the salt, Brother"—a precise system of gestures and sign language was used. The only monk who could speak was the rector in charge for the week. From his granite pulpit, he read sacred texts, the lives of the Fathers of the Church, without raising his voice, thanks to the extraordinary acoustics of the inverted keel vault: a sort of ceremony of sharing the fruits of the earth and the spirit, a communion of monks.

The dark days of the 14th century

The 14th century began with a bad omen: around 1300, the north tower of the church façade collapsed, destroying the priceless treasure of hundreds of manuscripts and works in the library learnedly put together from the abbotship of Torigni onward. In 1348 the Black Plague reduced the number of monks even further, just as the Hundred Years War, the civil war between Armagnacs and Burgundians, and the Great Schism of Western Christianity (Avignon/Rome) were getting underway. The madness of Charles VI completed the gloomy picture.

The Norman cathedrals and monasteries entrusted the mount with their well-filled caskets. The mount knew it was under threat—the English had an advanced post at Tombelaine, only 3 kilometres away (1356). The village armed itself and was equipped with a garrison and new fortifications in the 14th, 15th, and 16th centuries. From then on, it had three gates that were difficult to breach, as well as a long wall protecting the timber-frame dwellings. This wall, the curtain, was reinforced by about ten towers, some of which prefigured the designs of the military engineer and architect Vauban. A parapet walk went round all the ramparts; there was a single battlement so that the watch could mount guard there.

Bertrand Du Guesclin, constable of France, the second most important person in the kingdom, was a thorn in the sides of the English. Captain of Pontorson and guardian of the mount, he visited it several times. On the rock, the "Black Mastiff of Brocéliande" had a house built for his lady-love, Tiphaine de Raguenel, an astrologer and a bit of a witch.

The village's only street, a few hundred metres long, ended in the Escalier du Grand Degré Extérieur (Great Outer Staircase) leading to the abbey, which had a new entrance built to the east in around 1260. This building housed the Salle des Gardes and the lofty Belle-Chaise, the abbots' law courts. Fearing a siege, the abbey improved its defences around 1400: for example, the Tour Perrine, six floors for the men of arms. At the Grand Degré Extérieur, the abbey's new entrance was that of a citadel: barbican, portcullis falling between the two towers of the *châtelet* (outwork defending a thoroughfare), then steep stairs—the Gouffre—to the Salle des Gardes filtering all arrivals. In the early 15th century, the noose tightened, the English returned to camp at Tombelaine. The mount was the only stronghold that escaped the English.

Saint Michael, the celestial patriot

There was an unbelievable reversal of fortune in 1419: Abbot Jolivet, who had recently fortified the mount, defected to the enemy. He even came back to besiege his former flock—in vain, as his past fortifications proved to be effective. The traitor was so won over to the English cause that he, along with other Norman abbots, was an associate judge at the trial of Joan of Arc.

For a quarter of a century, the English wanted to put paid to the myth of the archangel protector of the mount and Charles VII, who was dazzled by the pugnacious defence of the mount's inhabitants. This recalls a certain village of indomitable Gauls that held out against the Roman invaders. The multiple English attacks failed—attacking a fortress whose boundless moat is filled twice a day by the tide was never going to be easy.

In 1434 the English nearly pulled it off. But the mount's inhabitants filled the breach opened by enemy bombards firing stone balls weighing up to 150 kilograms. The English sounded the retreat, abandoning two enormous cannons, the *michelettes*. These trophies still have pride of place near the entrance to the village, the Porte de l'Avancée.

The resistance to the armies of Henry V and later Henry VI gave the mount national hero status and Saint Michael the status of the saviour of the mount, and thus of the French kingdom. Popular songs bear witness to the resistance to the English occupation: "Between ourselves, villagers who love the French king, take heart every one of you, to fight the English." The mount's fame spread like wildfire. Inviolate, it became the symbol of a faltering national identity. The patriotism of revenge, after 1871 and before 1914, had its roots there. All the more so since in the late 19th century the rechristianisation undertaken by the Catholic Church gave a boost to pilgrimages and the cult of Saint Michael, patron saint of soldiers. In 1940–45, Marshal Pétain, a habitué of the mount and La Mère Poulard, was favourable to the cult of Saint Michael, a sort of nationalist takeover of "Army and Church".

The residence of Tiphaine, to the right of the parish church of Saint-Pierre and a little below the barbican (abbey entrance). This building is the oldest on the mount as, although extensively modified, it is thought to have been erected around 1365 by Bertrand Du Guesclin for his wife Tiphaine de Raguenel.

The new choir's cage of light

Around 1450, the war of well over a hundred years finally came to an end. Pilgrimages of thanksgiving multiplied. This revival brought a new prosperity to the abbey, which was, moreover, plied with gifts and tax exemptions granted by Charles VII, then by his son Louis XI. It was high time to rebuild the Romanesque choir that had collapsed in 1421. It was only around 1521–23—a century later—that this renaissance would be completed. The new choir is supported from below by a strange crypt with 10 stout pillars, 8 of which measured 7 metres high by 5.5 metres in circumference. The collapsed Romanesque choir's successor was in a Gothic style that was both sober and majestic, managing to steer clear of the exuberance of the "flamboyant" period. At the base: large pointed arches; above, the openwork triforium accentuates the springing up of the stone tracery. Higher above, the soaring upward movement is prolonged by narrow clerestory windows. Under the vault, the choir rises to a height of 25 metres, but appears much higher. Especially in the morning, it is a cage of light.

The grafting of the Gothic choir, with its vertical lines, on to the Romanesque nave, with its horizontal lines, was risky. Yet it came out all right in the end. There was no "break"; the marriage of granite worked.

The bell tower was rebuilt later and modified several times. The mount's silhouette only dates from 1897. Topped with a wooden vault rising to 17 metres, the Romanesque seven-bay nave is still intact. It almost disappeared in the 16th century, when there were plans to raze it and put up a Gothic nave.

The late 16th century saw the beginning of the abbey's decline, which had three causes: the decline of the order, pilgrimages marking time, and the conduct of the abbots who came from court, indifferent to their responsibilities but not to money. Appointed by the king from then on, usually through friendly contacts, the "commendatory" abbot no longer resided at the mount. If he did visit, it was to collect revenues. The abbey no longer had spiritual guide or financial steward. The impressive abbatial residences, built in the late 14th century, were soon used only to imprison the exiles of the "Bastille by the sea", after the delivery of a *lettre de cachet* (Louis XIV, Louis XV, Louis XVI).

Of reform

Tempted by the stronghold's location and the riches of the advanced post of the Holy League, the Huguenots tried desperately to invest it. They were led by the sons of Gabriel de Montgomery, the unwitting murderer of Henri II and later Protestant leader, who was beheaded in 1574. The Protestants, using trickery, went from failure to failure. In 1591 one of the many attempts on the mount ended in tragedy. Attracted to the ground floor of the Merveille by one of the inhabitants of the mount's counter-ruses, about a hundred swordsmen perished in a bloodbath, which is why the storeroom and the almonry were also known as *montgomeries*.

In the late 16th and early 17th centuries, the order fell to pieces. A few monks stayed at the mount, while others preferred the country and the priories of the coast. The problem was that these "men of letters" no longer knew Latin and Greek, and only just spoke French. Forgotten were the vow of chastity, the cowl, and the tonsure, to be replaced by long-haired, bearded men dressed in lace and silk. A few scoundrels brought women into the enclosure. Children born of sin played on the Grand Degré stairs. The village taverns cultivated drunkards. In the abbey, the doors no longer closed and the windows were half-open; the buildings were not maintained. The monastery ended up living from hand to mouth on the fees paid by the kings for their 150 residents, the "exiles".

In 1622 there were only sixteen monks left at the abbey. The mount was a pale shadow of its former self. This decay was intolerable in the eyes of the Benedictines of the congregation of Saint-Maur. They moved in to impose their reform. Young, austere, and learned, they re-established the order and were more interested in books and manuscripts than in architecture. They renovated the library of 4,000 works and made major changes to the halls so as to organise their own community life. The refectory was disfigured, becoming a dormitory with two levels; the Crypte de Notre-Dame-des-Trente-Cierges was used as a wine cellar. The most regrettable of these interventions was the so-called "classical" façade that the Maurists built in 1780 for the abbey church, whose first three bays and final Torigni tower had just been ruined by a fire. The Romantic writer Théophile Gautier called this rather uninspired replacement façade a "shopfront".

In the tradition of the Renaissance, the 18th century of the Enlightenment refused to continue to see the monks as the civilising force of days gone by: these contemplatives were of no use to society; the mount was nothing more than a Gothic wedding cake, the barbarian art of the obscurantist Middle Ages.

The mount's Benedictine saga ended with the fifty-first abbot, the Cardinal de Montmorency-Laval.

In which the mount is nothing but a prison

In 1790 the monastic orders were suppressed.

At the mount—dirty, dilapidated, more or less abandoned—the Revolution did not find many people: a few old monks, three forgotten prisoners, four screaming lunatics, and not much else. The looters of relics and reliquaries and the lovers of rare books had already called in. A total of 1.125 kilograms of gold and 25.35 kilograms of silver were salvaged—a meagre booty for an abbey that had long been used as a safe. As a bonus, the sans-culottes of Avranches seized three mitres—the abbots of the mount held the rank of bishop—and six bells, which were all melted down, except one, which continued to serve as a marker for walkers lost in the fog of the shore. The "Bastille by the sea" was not razed like the mother house in Paris. The former Mont-Michel became Mont-Libre and was once again transformed into a prison. The Revolution crammed its enemies in deplorable conditions: hundreds of non-juring priests, resistant to the Civil Constitution of the Clergy, then the Chouans, then the common-law criminals, one on top of the other. One can just imagine the group photo. Under Napoleon, the situation got worse: the abbey was decreed a prison. The Restoration added two "house specialities": hard labour for men and women, and a reformatory for eighty children. A sojourn that surely restored them. All the openings were secured with bars. Most of the spaces, including the church, were converted into dormitories, mills, or straw hat or shoe workshops. The mount had over 700 prisoners, including elderly convicts and future deportees. From 1830, they were joined by legitimists, democrats, and famous republicans, such as Louis Auguste Blanqui and Armand Barbès,

shut up in horrible dungeons, as they had made several failed escape attempts.

A member of the Monuments Historiques inventory team in 1836, Victor Hugo visited the mount, with its splendours and horrors. He left disgusted: "It's a toad in a reliquary." The prison-ants' nest was an insalubrious nightmare: 457 deaths, mainly from tuberculosis, from 1820 to 1830.

In the end, the dreadful prison, in which about 14,000 prisoners did time during the 19th century, roused the indignation of public opinion and the deputies. Napoleon III had it shut down in 1863 despite the petitions of the mount's inhabitants, for whom it provided a living. In 1850 the mount employed hundreds of guards and soldiers. The population (prisoners included) then numbered 1,182, but dropped, after the prison was closed, to 203 in 1866.

Restoration and interpretation

Paradoxically, the mount's use as a prison both damaged and saved it. However, its last days would have been wretched—an open-pit quarry serving as a perch for the seagulls—if the stars of Romanticism had not come to its rescue. The famous talents were sensitive to the medieval heritage.

The military engineer Vauban, disappointed by his inspection of the mount's so-called stronghold in 1691, produced this realistically detailed model of the mount. The remarkable piece of work dates from 1701. Village, ramparts, and towers are depicted in minute detail, including some of the furniture. Note the surviving Romanesque tower, one of the two towers on either side of the abbey church façade that Abbot Robert de Torigni had built in the 12th century (Paris, Musée des Plans-Reliefs).

First to arrive, the architect Viollet-le-Duc was only twenty-one in 1835 when he discovered the extent of the damage. Struck by "the beauty of this pile of stones", he left with eleven watercolours, wash drawings, and plans for a spire. Hugo followed him, then, in no particular order, Flaubert, Jules Michelet, Stendhal, Prosper Mérimée, head of the Monuments Historiques in 1841, and even Guy de Maupassant. Gautier became an admirer of the mount, his description attracting considerable attention: "All this architecture soars upward with an ardour for climbing that the centuries have not cooled and seems to want to take by storm the mountain it covers."

The hoped-for decision came in 1874: the listing as a historical monument. Ready to get on with the job for two years, the main architect of the restoration, Édouard Corroyer (who arrived with his maid, the future Mère Poulard), did not know where to start, so much was there to be done. In 1879, while he fought with

the Ponts and Chaussées civil engineering body (builders of the causeway, which unwisely ended between two of the ramparts' towers), Corroyer reinforced everything he could, for example, the cloister. As a worthy pupil of Viollet-le-Duc, he adhered to the master's doctrine of unity of style: "To restore an edifice means neither to maintain it, nor to repair it, nor to rebuild it; it means to re-establish it in a finished state, which may in fact never have actually existed at any given time." This amounts to saying that Viollet-le-Duc did not want to restore the monument to its original state but to the state it should be in, at least in his eyes: the "Violletist" architects sought consistency with their own image of the Middle Ages. Hence the interpretations, excesses, and deviations. Thus, Corroyer allowed himself to add "picturesque" crenellations on the upper section of the Merveille, on all of the north façade. Later, particularly Paul Gout and Yves-Marie Froidevaux, who wanted to leave traces of history, architect

This finely observed drawing of the choir's flying buttresses is by the young architect Eugène Viollet-le-Duc, who first visited the mount in 1835. Viollet-le-Duc and Victor Hugo were the first militants for the abbey's restoration. Drawing, pen and ink, and watercolour (Paris, MAP, Geneviève Viollet-le-Duc collection).

In the name of the doctrine of unity of style, and thus of the monument, this restoration project envisaged tearing down the Gothic choir to reinstall the Romanesque choir. In the 16th century, there were plans to demolish the Romanesque nave to replace it with a Gothic one. Watercolour drawing by Émile Sagot, c. 1875 (Paris, MAP).

In 1872 Édouard Corroyer, sent at the suggestion of Viollet-le-Duc, arrived at the mount with his convictions, including that of the monument's unity of style. In addition to his restoration projects (scaffolding on the refectory), he added the battlements of a medieval chateau to the top of the Merveille's north façade (Paris, MAP).

Drawn in the late 19th century, the mount seen (from left to right and from top to bottom) from the east, west, north, and south. At the time, many and varied restoration projects were envisaged. The architect Édouard Corroyer planned to rebuild the three missing Romanesque bays of the church and put back the two towers of its façade that Abbot Torigni had built in the past. Drawings by Édouard Corroyer, pen and ink and watercolour, 1873 (Paris, MAP).

Take binoculars

The restoration laboratory that the mount had become ended up resembling the famed *Très Riches Heures du duc de Berry* (first half of the 15th century): that is, a somewhat idealised image of the Middle Ages.

Mont-Saint-Michel is one of the most beautiful landscapes of sky, earth, and sea. It stands out against its surroundings in the style of Turner, a theatrical matinee in the style of Victor Hugo, with a soundtrack of passionate music by Richard Wagner. It is a promise that keeps its promises.

After having climbed the hundreds of rough granite steps and reached the terrace level with the square in front of the abbey church, take time to take in the seascapes. South of nearby Mont-Dol are Brittany and the polders; to the west, the English Channel, far behind the vast grey-blue bay, with perhaps a few indolent seals; to the north, Tombelaine the silent, the salt marshes, and the River Cotentin.

Mont-Saint-Michel, at risk from the sea, is a giant sundial. On the infinite shores that surround it, the shadow of the church spire slowly turns—to show the course of the sun, all the horizons, and to make you dream.

The heritage belongs to the beholder.

In around 1600 a booklet printed by the monks recounted the history of the mount and included practical information. The year 1866 saw the publication of *Voyage au Mont-Saint-Michel*, the first guide with photographs for those who went on excursions to the mount. In 1872 the railway came to Pontorson from where, in 1901, the steam tram set out to the foot of the mount. In 1890 the Chemins de Fer de l'Ouest railway offered leisure trains with reduced fares. Guides by the architect and restorer Paul Gout were published in 1906 and 1921 (Paris, MAP).

Stretching over the infinite sand, the mount is transformed by the course of the sun into a giant sundial. On the right, the silhouette that appears suddenly is no cause for worry: it is a sardonic gargoyle, one of the sentinels of rain perched at a right angle above the abbey's vertiginous heights.

restorers were more respectful of authenticity. The most blatant "interpretation" involved the present abbey church bell tower. In 1897 the architect Victor Petitgrand replaced it with a Neo-Romanesque tower topped with a 32-metre Gothic Revival spire. The resemblance to the one recently restored by Viollet-le-Duc, his former master, for Notre-Dame de Paris is clear. Petitgrand wanted to top his new spire with a new statue of Saint Michael because his sources referred to a gilt one in the 16th century. The French Republic heeded him, allowing itself the luxury of commissioning from the sculptor Emmanuel Frémiet a Saint Michael in copper gilt over 4 metres tall. A motionless traveller in the clouds, the triumphant archangel tramples Beelzebub, the fallen angel, underfoot in the style of Raphael. The Prince of the Heavenly Hosts has since been inseparable from the world-renowned silhouette of Mont-Saint-Michel.

A CLOSER LOOK

On the Breton horizon—
salt marshes in front
of polders protected
by a dyke—is the sacred
enclosure on its granite
pedestal. A crown of ridges
suspended in midair,
the mount is an act
of love involving sky,
sea, and architecture.

As the seagull flies:
the mount from the west,
with the classical-style façade
of the abbey church, and
in front of it the huge terrace
that allows one to admire
Tombelaine, the River Cotentin,
the distant Channel, and the
Chausey Islands when they
choose to reveal themselves.
From the south terrace,

there are views over Brittany
and Mont-Dol (63 metres),
the third granitic mound,
surrounded by earth and
marshes since antiquity.
The commune of Mont-
Saint-Michel, founded in 1790,
is not limited to the mount's
2 hectares; it also comprises
397 hectares of agricultural
land on the mainland.

Surrounded by its medieval ramparts, the mount is an incredible concentration of civilisation—and tourism. The constraint that builders have had to deal with for centuries is immediately apparent: constructing an abbey church on the narrow summit, the monastery buildings, including the Merveille, on the sides of the summit, and the other buildings around the rock. Hence the strange configuration of edifices on the sugar loaf mountain rising out of the bay's 40,000 hectares.
On the horizon is the islet of Tombelaine in front of the Cotentin's Norman bank.

The *tangue* (the sand of the bay) encircles the mount a little more each year.
The salt marshes, native pastures, are colonising the former mud flats: 20–40 additional hectares each year. It is the preserve of 10,000–15,000 salt meadow sheep, a local breed with black heads and legs. Launched, like the omelette, by the renown of Mère Poulard's inn, the roast leg of lamb is of great repute thanks to the diet of the animals, who graze on grass flooded two or three times a month by the spring tides.

The saying "If you go to the mount, confess your sins and draw up your will" dates from the time when the Heavenly Jerusalem could only be reached on foot at low tide. Nonetheless the bay's four dangers still exist: fog, lightning, the tides, and quicksand, the age-old fear. You think that the surface is dry and that you are walking on solid ground: it's an illusion, only a film covering an unfathomable pocket of silt filled with water. In the words of Victor Hugo: "The wretched man tries to sit down, to lie down, to climb; every movement that he makes buries him deeper; he straightens himself up, he sinks; he feels that he is being swallowed up; he shrieks, implores, cries to the clouds, wrings his hands, grows desperate. Behold him in the sand up to his belly, the sand reaches to his breast, he is only a bust now. He uplifts his hands . . . clenches his nails on the beach, tries to cling fast to that ashes, supports himself on his elbows in order to raise himself from that soft sheath, and sobs frantically; the sand mounts higher. The sand has reached his shoulders, the sand reaches to his throat; only his face is visible now. His mouth cries aloud, the sand fills it; silence. . . . Sinister obliteration of a man."
Les Misérables, trans. by Isabel Florence Hapgood (New York: Thomas Y. Crowell & Co., 1887).

To replace a few rudimentary wooden "pickets", the mount had more effective protection built for itself in the 13th century: a wall on the edge of the shore linked the village's few dozen houses. As the conflicts drew near, the mount equipped itself with real ramparts: a long, high wall connecting several towers. The Hundred Years War speeded up the work on the fortifications, the abbey included.
Louis XI, very attached to Mont-Saint-Michel, financed its militarisation. Three new towers were built around 1480, including the Tour Boucle. In this photo, one can locate the large Tour Boucle, which prefigured Vauban's designs. Jutting out 20 metres over the eastern shoreline, its walls (4 metres thick) shelter 4 storeys with embrasures for wrought-iron *veuglaires* (guns) that were very advanced for the period as they were breechloaders. A seemingly incredible detail: the ramparts and towers were built on sand. Their foundations rested on the *tangue* to a depth of 5–7 metres. When *tangue* is really dry, especially deep down, it becomes concrete footing.

The Tour Gabriel was designed by Captain Gabriel du Puy de Murinais in 1524. This bastion, 16 metres in diameter and equipped with some 15 embrasures, allowed weapons to be fired in all directions. Placed on the left ledge, a watch turret was used to keep watch on the horizon safe from musket shot. At the top, the small tower with a pepperpot roof is a windmill added in the 18th century. It was used as a lighthouse in the 19th century.

Without this tangle of flying buttresses and counter-forts, with their pinnacles, reinforcing the walls of the choir, it would collapse, knocked over by its lateral forces.

The apse of the granite gem is thus a triumph of balance between the masonry and the light, slender walls. With its luxuriant stone, the flamboyant style was a dying spark of the Middle Ages since the choir was completed in 1523, while the Renaissance was already in full bloom.

Above the abbatial residences, between the flying buttresses and the nave of the abbey church, is the south transept. Unlike the shortened north transept, modified in the 13th century to accommodate the cloister, the south transept is intact. It long housed the Trinity altar, where the principal relics were venerated.

Let's read this photo from right to left.

To the right, halfway up the hill, is the low Tour Claudine, which was used to store gunpowder and munitions. It dominated the stairhead of the Escalier du Grand Degré Extérieur.

To its left: the crenellated barbican, dominated by the two cylindrical towers of the *châtelet*, the pointed Tour des Corbins (Crow Tower), connecting the three floors of the Merveille, with its A-frame roof.

In the centre: the Belle-Chaise with its narrow clerestory windows and the ground-floor Salle des Gardes. To its left: the Tour Perrine, six floors that housed a garrison (Hundred Years War) under the command of the man who had the tower built, Abbot Pierre Le Roy. After that is the bailiwick, set back a little. Finally, the lofty building housing the abbatial residences and its powerful counter-forts.

In the foreground, the bell tower of the parish church of Saint-Pierre. This Romanesque sanctuary was said to have been founded on Bishop Aubert's wishes. Mentioned in a 1022 deed, the church was extensively modified, particularly in the 15th and 16th centuries. Since 1886, it has housed the mount's pilgrimage centre.

Beyond the barbican: the *châtelet* with its two towers. Between these "cannon shafts" is the Gouffre, a formidably steep staircase. If the new arrival was an assailant, a portcullis would fall in front of his face and blunt objects hit him on the back of the head. Every visitor, unless he was a prince of the blood, had to leave his arms in the Salle des Gardes, which had a heavy door. The whole of this obligatory route was cheerfully named the Assommoir (murder hole).

Overhung by two internal circulation bridges, the Grand Degré Intérieur staircase, with its processional landings, leads to the abbey church and west terrace.

In the Gothic style, fairly thin walls had a natural tendency to be out of plumb. As there was a risk of collapse, there were finely worked intersecting supports: flying buttresses, like stone bridges starting at the counter-forts, span the void to support the sides of the choir. On top of the counter-forts, pointed pinnacles play a double role: an aesthetic function, to accentuate the impression of height, and that of weight, securing the masonry that they top. The flamboyant technique brought the Gothic style to its zenith. That is why we praise it to the skies.

Above

The lacework stairs
were put up on the back
of the "slope" of a flying
buttress than spans the void
between a counter-fort that
is sturdier that the others
and the gallery encircling
the choir roof.
This close-up shows
its exceptional balustrade,
carved in the 16th century.
It was long rumoured that
the sculptor of this Gothic
masterpiece was a prisoner
named Gaultier, who was
said to have killed himself
by jumping from the top
of one of the mount's
platforms.

Following pages

This daring photo, taken
from the top of the spire,
looks over the choir
and south transept
to the right, the village
below, and the shore
on a day of spring tides.
The points of light are
floodlights. This aerial shot
affords a view of the forest
of flying buttresses
surrounding the bell tower
with its double-tiered crown
of pointed pinnacles
launching an attack on
the apse roof.

The first three Romanesque bays (there were seven originally) of the 11th-century church collapsed during the mount's eleventh fire in 1776. Their collapse led to that of the surviving tower (on the right) of the two Robert de Torigni had built in the 12th century.
So, in 1780, the Maurist monks put up this austere façade, called "classical", which somewhat recalled the Jesuit "style".
To the left: the former dormitory housing one of the abbey's two bookshops. The Maurists lacked means and a taste for architecture. Théophile Gautier, who was passionately fond of the mount, called the façade a "shopfront". Fortunately, at this spot, the spectacle is elsewhere, with the views from the west terrace, built on the site of the three bays destroyed by fire.

The Romanesque main north-south stairs.

The church of Notre-Dame-sous-Terre. In the background, the roughly dressed large blocks make us hopeful that they are the traces of the first artificial grotto dedicated to Saint Michael by Bishop Aubert. Note the Carolingian bricks of the arches and the former gallery of relics above the dressed stones.

The monks' ambulatory is a blend of two styles. It is proof of the arrival of the Gothic style at the mount. It took place in three stages. First, the long hall, divided by five columns and able to accommodate about fifty people, was built in the 11th century with a rustic wooden ceiling. After the collapse of the north wall of the church nave and the fire of 1112, a groined vault with transverse arches was put up. The third phase, which resulted in the space's present appearance, was a restoration during the 12th century: an intersecting rib vault over the columns and Romanesque walls was erected. As a result, the arches were embedded into the wall with difficulty. It hard to think of this austere space as an ambulatory.

The Maurist monks, masters of the mount from the 17th century, didn't ask themselves any questions—they used the supposed ambulatory for their latrines.

The Salle de l'Aquilon used to be near the first north-west entrance of the Romanesque abbey—hence the name Aquilon, a formidably cold north wind. This was where thousands of pilgrims who had just crossed the strand were welcomed. Dating from the 11th century, the Aquilon is divided into two naves by three stout columns. Stone groined vaults were added in the 12th century. If you look closely, you can see traces of the formwork—the savoir-faire of the 1100s.

The blocks, reddish in colour as a result of the fire of 1834, would have been replaced with new granite ones by the two first restorers. The third architect, Paul Gout, wanted to maintain the traces of the passage of history.

He thus kept the reddened blocks: "All stones are equally respectable . . . the systematic pursuit of unity [of style, Viollet-le-Duc's concept] leads to the tearing of interesting pages out of the book made up by the monument on the pretext that they are not written with the same characters."

It's unlikely that Gout's ideas would have been accepted by all of his contemporaries.

In 1521 the old nave was married to a young flamboyant choir. Gustave Flaubert (1847) approved of this graft: "The church has a Gothic choir and a Romanesque nave, which seem to vie with each other in majesty and elegance."

The Romanesque masonry was thick and ponderous. Before it was restored, it was sometimes unstable, and even incapable of supporting a vault.

For the ceiling, 17 metres high, the traditional Norman wooden barrel vault was used.

Structural weaknesses led to several collapses, for example, that of the north side of the nave onto the monks' dormitory in 1103. The monks, thank heavens, were at matins at the time. Incredibly, in the 16th century, the Romanesque nave was almost demolished. Filled with enthusiasm by the success of the flamboyant choir, the abbots imagined an abbey church entirely in the choir's image.

If you look at the south side of the apse, you'll see the beginning of arches. Works to make the church "entirely Gothic" had well and truly got underway.

The Gothic choir reaches 25 metres at its highest point. The final vault is decorated with keystones bearing the coat of arms of Abbot Jean III de Lamps, who completed work on the new choir. Other shields may be recognised, such as that of Abbot Jean IV le Veneur, who was host to François I. "Return of the Romanesque": in the late 19th century, the abbey church was almost entirely redone in Romanesque style. In line with the tenets of Viollet-le-Duc, the mount's first two restorers wanted to destroy all that was Gothic in the church to get back to the entirely Romanesque sanctuary, including the three bays that had disappeared in the fire of 1776.
It would have been a Neo-Romanesque clone, true to the famous miniature in *Les Très Riches Heures du duc de Berry*—a hair's breadth from total contempt for the passage of history.

"Be watchers-awakeners," said Cardinal Marty at the time of the foundation of the Monastic Fraternities of Jerusalem at the church of Saint-Gervais, Paris, in 1975. Since 2001, at the mount, the spiritual renewal of the Heavenly Jerusalem has been represented by half a dozen nuns and about as many monks, all dressed in cream-white. Their prioress and prior are permanent residents of "the mount of prayer", as the medieval monks would have said. On the other hand, the sisters and brothers alternate—a few weeks or months, or even a year—between contemplative life in the abbey and paid working life, often far from the mount. Part-time between God and job, like "Jesus going from town to town on His way to Jerusalem". The two autonomous communities live separately, only the liturgy brings them together—for example, in the above photo, for the midday service often attended by visitors, whether they are believers or not. Moreover, it is possible to make a spiritual retreat at the abbey, on weekdays, thanks to a few guestrooms. For these nuns and monks, it is a praying immersion in the passing crowd, "an itinerant city". The vocation of the Monastic Fraternities of Jerusalem is to promote the spirit of the monastic wilderness in the heart of the city through the beauty of the liturgy. An oasis of prayer where everyone may come to recharge his or her batteries.

The south transept of the abbey church is supported by the Crypte de Saint-Martin and its exceptional 9-metre transverse arch.

The Crypte des Gros Piliers: the two "palm-tree" pillars in the centre are characteristic—like the eight other, much stouter ones—of the flamboyant Gothic style. The ten original Romanesque pillars had collapsed at the same time as the Romanesque choir that they supported in 1421. The reconstruction of this crypt, from 1446 to 1452, provided the new underground support for Gothic choir, which was completed in 1521–23. The technique used for this crypt was amazing, particularly the precise fitting of the prismatic profile of the ribs of the arching and their penetration of the column shafts.

An admirable success given the modest materials that the caste of architects and stonecutters had at its disposal. Fortunately, these masters became more confident and experienced with each project. They became experts at calculating loads, weights, and thrusts.

From the start, the Crypte des Gros Piliers, built beginning in 1023, supported the choir of the abbey church. But the church collapsed in 1421 because the underground columns were not solid enough to withstand the enormous weight of the Romanesque masonry. From 1446 to 1452, the crypt was rebuilt on the salvageable old pillars.

A few of them were probably contained within the much more imposing new pillars, especially 8 of them, which were 7 metres high and 5.5 metres in circumference. The ten pillars together were meant to support the new Gothic choir on the floor above. Unlike the church's two other crypts, under the north and south transepts, the Crypte des Gros Piliers was probably never used for worship.

This somewhat oppressive space served as a crossroads at the heart of the abbey.

It was also used as an antechamber for the mount's law court, the nearby Belle-Chaise. Some of those awaiting trial must have spent an agonising wait there, all the more so given the decor.

The cloister's west wall: the three openings attest to plans to extend the Merveille by adding a third main block. To the left, the charter room added in the late 14th or early 15th century. Abbot Pierre Le Roy, a European specialist in canon law, had this square tower built. The charter room has long housed the considerable collection of *chartes*, the abbey's title deeds, which could be consulted on the premises. Sadly, these priceless documents were destroyed during the Normandy landings of 1944.

"Nearness to the sea destroys pettiness." (Stendhal) This exceptional view is through the three openings made in the cloister's west wall in the past. It was here that the monks could have entered on the same level as the chapter house at the top of the third building planned for the Merveille. But the project—outlined by the ambitious Abbot Richard II Turstin—was abandoned in favour of other programmes of works on the mount, including the abbey's new east entrance, a complete overhaul of the circulation of pilgrims and monks (*c.* 1260). Several architects and restorers were sensitive to the romantic charm of the three windows and their views, particularly at the end of the day. There were many attempts to set them off, notably with iron glazed sashes; then, in 1934, Ernest Herpe had large panes of glass set in copper frames put in; Yves-Marie Froidevaux opted for these very simple large openings in the 1960s. Take the time to look at the shoreline made iridescent by the setting sun.

The westernmost point of the Merveille. To the right, the reinforced vertical wall of the counter-forts of the abbey church's north transept. In the foreground, the pointed gable roof of the former monks' dormitory, now one of the abbey's two bookshops. In the background: the refectory's west façade with its large Gothic window. Above it are the two fireplaces of the Salle des Hôtes on the second level underneath the refectory. The pointed tower, with the bay behind it, contains a spiral staircase connecting the floors of the Merveille. The thick walls contain networks of secret passages, which proved very useful during the many sieges.

One of the highlights of the Merveille: the refectory tops the eastern section of the building, above the Salle des Hôtes. Amongst the seventy-three chapters of the rule is one that required the "black monks" of the Familia (the original name for a Benedictine monastery) to make use of only the light that God provided, whatever the season. So, in the early 13th century, the master builder designed a clever and discreet system to light this space: fifty-nine narrow windows are concealed between the small columns of the north and south façades, hence the evenly distributed light.

"Art is a way of pleasing God."
The Gothic style fulfils this duty perfectly. Clinging to the north side of the mount, the Merveille houses six magnificent spaces in two buildings. In the western building is the Salle des Chevaliers, which was probably never frequented by knights, except perhaps the 119 who had taken part in the mount's defence during the Hundred Years War. The name may be due to the founding—but in Amboise—of the Order of Saint Michael by Louis XI. The pious king, a regular visitor of the mount, had a soft spot for the archangel. Robustness prevailed over elegance.

With some grandeur, this space is divided into four naves by three rows of columns, the last of which, on the south side, clings to the rock. The arches of the vaulting are more pointed than those of the adjacent Salle des Hôtes. The sculpted decoration of the baskets of the squat capitals features "luxuriant foliage" reminiscent of the Norman motifs of the cathedral of Coutances.
The Salle des Chevaliers is the largest room in the abbey and the least uncomfortable. It had latrines (in the counter-forts of the north wall) and two huge fireplaces with oblique mantels, which rise to the

vaulting. Fitted out on the north side, these fireplaces spared the monk copyists and illuminators from having hands numb with cold and from dipping their quills into frozen ink.
The room was also divided into small separate spaces with tapestries. The golden age of Mont-Saint-Michel's Romanesque scriptorium was between 1050 and 1080: we do not know where it was located. When the Gothic Salle des Chevaliers was born, the decline of the scriptorium had already began as a result of competition from urban lay workshops. Therefore, if the scriptorium had indeed been located in this place, it must have

been only for a very short time. We suspect that this Salle des Chevaliers was used as the need arose: scriptorium, warming room, community space, chapter, or even library or place for consultation since one of the room's doors opens on to the tower of the charter room in the north-west corner. Moreover, great care was taken to allow in natural light, with a large window in the west wall and a series of round windows, oculi, in the north wall: "The circle, that is, an image of circular time, a perfect and infinite line, and thus the clearest symbol of eternity," wrote medievalist Georges Duby.

Intended for distinguished pilgrims, the elegant Salle des Hôtes is in the Île-de-France style.
It is a demonstration of the Gothic technique designed to stay in the memory of visitors so that they could help attract many others. The prestigious space played this role so well that distinguished figures flocked to it. Saint Louis was the guest of honour at two major receptions in this space adorned with stained-glass windows, tapestries, paintings, and tiles decorated with the arms of France and Blanche de Castille. According to legend, Louis IX, out of humility, was said not to have taken part in the feast and preferred to go up a floor to share the earthly and spiritual nourishment of the monks in the refectory.
In the Salle des Hôtes, everything was on hand for the comfort of crowned and mitred heads.
Thus the kitchen was near to the twin fireplaces.
In these huge hearths, entire animals were roasted, from snout (*barbe*) to tail (*cul*), hence the word "barbecue".

Right-hand page

The cloister's garden existence fluctuated: had it even been laid out in 1230? At the very beginning of the 17th century, it was thought to have made an appearance, but was removed because of leaks on the floor below (Salle des Chevaliers). Restored in 1623, it was removed again in 1676 because of recurrent leaks despite attempts to make it watertight with lead plates. It was not until the architect Froidevaux installed a concrete slab (1965) that Father Bruno de Senneville was able to redesign an austere garden (1966).

The cloister, a bridge between heaven and earth. Around the garden, the gallery is supported by 137 small columns in superb "crimson pudding stone" from Lucerne d'Outre-Mer, Granville. The rhythm of the small columns "rounded off" the corners so well that the gallery formed a pathway in which it was possible to walk and meditate without having to worry about the weather or the passing time. The inner small columns support arches in Caen stone decorated with symbols and figures: Christ, Saint Francis, a grape picker (perhaps Noah), and even a dragon representing the Devil, always trying to lead into temptation. The plant-like friezes and floral garlands, real stone lacework, exalt the abundance of Creation, the dynamism of life, and the earthly paradise to be refound. When the monks raised their eyes, the pages of the stone book turned with every footstep.

At night, it is easier to appreciate the mount's new vertical thrust, a result of the recasting of the clock tower in 1897: a Neo-Romanesque tower with a Gothic Revival spire, similar to the lead spire the architect Viollet-le-Duc had recently added for his restoration of Notre-Dame de Paris. This new silhouette was the image of the mount that would henceforth circulate around the world. The mount was almost completely abandoned after the prison was closed (1863). It had, moreover, become a shadow of its former self, so severe was the damage. Fortunately, people began taking interest in medieval heritage, once completely disparaged, in around 1830. Viollet-le-Duc first visited Mont-Saint-Michel in 1835 and expressed his admiration for the mount in general and the abbey in particular. Much criticised —criticism that was often justified—he is now a little better understood. He was greatly blamed for his intransigence about his doctrine regarding the unity of style of the monument in relation to the original structure.
This led him to deviations, interpretations, and excess. However, Viollet-le-Duc, who advocated the use of metal before Gustave Eiffel, is not without merit. What would Notre-Dame de Paris, the basilicas of Vézelay and Saint-Denis, the Cité de Carcassonne, the Palais des Papes in Avignon, and even Mont-Saint-Michel have become without him? Perhaps not much, perhaps ruins slowly falling into neglect and consequently too expensive to restore.

IN DEPTH

Scriptorium and Scriptorial

"C'est un travail de bénédictin!" (It's a job fit for a Benedictine: that is, a painstaking task.) The French expression has survived from the time of monks working as copyists and illuminators with patience and talent to compile, transcribe, and illuminate precious manuscripts. During the Middle Ages, religious and profane works, produced in-house or acquired, and organised in a library, brought many readers to the mount. In the 21st century, the whole world marvels at these exceptional documents. We may admire some 200 survivors of the mount's scriptorium or other workshops at the Scriptorial d'Avranches.

From its foundation in 966, the monastery was richly endowed by the dukes of Normandy, then by monarchs, notably the kings of England. As a result, a scriptorium used by learned monks of noble birth was created. "Pray and work" was the motto of the Benedictine copyists who beautified the word of God. Very soon, it was necessary to add illustrations, illuminations (*illuminare*, "to light up" in Latin), and later miniatures (from *minium*, "red"). The sacred texts gave the four Fathers of the Church their due: lives and doctrines of Saint Augustine, Saint Ambrose, Saint Jerome, and Saint Gregory the Great. Exchanges began with other men of letters, from Canterbury, for example. The spiritual quest was also interested in knowledge. These scribes thus began their mission to transmit the classics, knowledge, and the works of contemporary authors. Today, these copyists would be computer scientists. Thus, from the 9th century, the mount's library safeguarded a copy of *De oratore* by the Roman Cicero in order to cultivate the purity of the Latin. Dating from the same period, around 850, the manuscript recounting the creation (in 708) of the sanctuary of the archangel was recopied in around 1000. This was fortunate as the 9th-century original has been lost forever.

The scriptorium's golden age was around 1050–75. Reading and writing being a form of prayer in the shadowy light and chilly damp, indeed, even by the flickering light of oil lamps (spectacles beginning in the 14th century), the monks wrote in Latin and cursive Caroline (Carolingian), the precursor of our handwriting. Goose, swan, and eagle quills were used. The ink was wood cinder-based or lamp-black; honey and gum arabic were used as binders. The delicate colours were minerals or ground plant materials bound with resin or egg white. The support, prepared using a pumice stone, was usually parchment, from the skins of the sheep of the bay's salt marshes, more rarely ass's skin or calfskin (vellum). The monks bent over the manuscripts for four hours a day to produce four pages on average. The work took weeks, months, a year. The paintings, produced using a brush (gouache, wash), were often by the text copyist. The scriptorium aimed for perfection, more in terms of quality than of originality. It became known for its creation of the "mount decorated initial", the first letter of the first word of the book or chapter to attract the reader's attention or inspire meditation. These initials became famous for their astounding decorative inventiveness: inhabited flourishes, fantastic animals, interlaced foliage, etc. The charm of the mount's work lay in a savoir-faire that was both elaborate and simple, resulting in elegant gaiety. It was soon succeeded by the historiated initial, with real or symbolised figures. Gothic illuminations, from the 13th century, were more realistic, with a sense of movement, a hint of emotion. We know eleven of the renowned scriptorium's leading lights. Those who dared to transgress humility *gratis pro Deo*. Let us quote Fromond, who reveals his identity at the end of a large volume entirely in his hand. A confession that is both immodest and funny:

> Long live the hand that
> applies itself to write so well.
> If someone is the copyist,
> you seek, dear reader,
> to find out who it is.
> It is Fromond, who,
> with zeal, wrote the book
> from start to finish.
> What he transcribed
> is very considerable.
> Only pious deeds
> has he thus completed!
> Happy Fromond,
> there is a brother that should
> be loved forever!

A cloister with no library is like an army with no arsenal

Already well-stocked in the 11th century, the mount's library took on a European scale in the 12th century with Robert de Torigni. The powerful abbot built its myth thanks to his passion for great literature and bibliophilism. He put his copyists to work, and used earlier and contemporary sources (some called him a mere compiler) to draft his chronicle, which was celebrated in the Middle Ages because of its universal character: the abbot began his narrative with Saint Jerome and ended it with his own era. It thus covered current events, including those in Normandy. At the same time, Torigni finished the magnificent cartulary, a collection of all the accounts of

The initial F of "Faustus". Saint Augustine, *Contra Faustum*, before 1060, by the monk Giraud. The line and range of colours are typical of the mount's scriptorium: this manuscript recounts the courteous debate between the bishop of Hippo and Faustus the Manichaean, upholder of the principle of good and evil, without nuance (Avranches, Bibliothèque Municipale, ms. 90, fol. 2).

Historiated initial of "*primus*". Eusebius of Caesarea, *Chronique de Robert de Torigni*, compiled between 1150 and 1186. The anonymous copyist uses the style and bestiary of the mount's cartulary. This illustration, as often in the chronicle, honours the work of the writer, for example Sigebert of Gembloux, himself the author of a famous historical chronicle during the Middle Ages. In the right hand of the scribe is his quill; in his left hand, a knife to remove blots (Avranches, Bibliothèque Municipale, ms. 159, fol. 7 verso).

the foundation of the abbey and inventory of all its possessions, to glorify its memory. The undertaking proved to be even more useful when 3,000 of the monastery's original charters went up in smoke after the bombing of Saint-Lô on 6 June 1944. Moreover, Torigni encouraged a "trouvère" monk from his team, Guillaume de Saint Pair, to write *Le Roman du Mont-Saint-Michel* in Vulgar Latin, which was more accessible. The work was 3,781 verses long and highlighted the sanctuary's origins in the dream of Aubert. Moreover, Torigni, curious and passionately interested in everything, began to diversify the library. Until then,

it contained mainly texts on theology, the liturgy, meditation, Gregorian chant, etc. The moralist Saint Augustine had pride of place: thirty treatises with four full-page images of him, and just three of the local hero, Saint Michael. With Torigni, the monastery began to open up to the outside world, a process that later accelerated, with a sort of encyclopedia collecting the knowledge accumulated since antiquity: mathematics, geometry, astronomy, medicine, law (the Code of Justinian), history, and even a strange treatise on music by Boethius transmitting the legacy of Pythagoras and the calculation of ideal numerical

proportions, long before the appearance of notes. Readers came from far and wide to consult these works, especially the books on literature, philosophy, rhetoric, and grammar. There were copies of works by Plato (12th century), Seneca, Pliny, Ovid, and, above all, Aristotle's treatise on logic. Between the in-house production and the growing number of acquisitions, Torigni was thought to have gathered together 140 works. This library was housed in one of the two towers (the Tour de l'Horloge, to the left) that he had built on either side of the abbey church façade. The tower collapsed in 1300, destroying nearly all of the rich collection put together by Torigni and his successors—probably hundreds of manuscripts.

Mont-Saint-Michel's 203 surviving manuscripts

The light of the outstanding scriptorium slowly faded in the 13th century with the emergence of the Gothic style and especially the competition from urban lay workshops (Sorbonne, 1257) and excellent itinerant copyists and illuminators. From then on, the monks of Mont-Saint-Michel travelled more often and returned laden with manuscripts, while the novices back from their studies (Collège du Mont, Paris) did the same with other contributions. The mount was enriched, for example, by the decretals of Pope Gregory IX and a splendid Bible

undoubtedly produced and illuminated in Paris. At the end of the Middle Ages (1453) the mount's library contained up to 800 manuscripts. In 1791 the monastery's collection of 4,000 volumes, a majority of which were printed books, was allocated to the municipality of Avranches, 20 kilometres from the mount. The treasures included a copy (*c.* 1000) by the monk Hervard of the original *Revelatio* (9th century), now missing; the cartulary (12th century), a lengthy manuscript finished under the supervision of Robert de Torigni; the so-called "Bible de Paris" (13th century): 1,200 pages, 2 volumes by the same scribe, 84 historiated initials; the beautifully illustrated decretals (canon law) of Gregory IX (1230, Padua, Italy); several manuscripts concerning Saint Augustine, the Doctor of Grace; Aristotle: precious documents from the 10th to the 14th century; and fragments of an Evangel that the abbey possessed in the 8th century.

The display case of the Scriptorial is a motionless but unforgettable voyage amongst the evidence of the spiritual, artistic, intellectual, and scientific ferment of the Middle Ages, considered obscurantist for far too long.

The temptation of Tombelaine

A strange, desolate place with the silhouette of a sphinx, the head being the knoll known as La Folie, 47 metres, Tombelaine has nevertheless attracted a lot of people. This granite islet, 3 kilometres north of Mont-Saint-Michel, has had an eventful history. Since 1985 it has been a bird sanctuary, off limits from 15 March to 15 July (nesting). After a few hermits in the first Christian centuries of Normandy, the 11th century and the intellectual ferment of the mount saw a few long stays by scholarly monks seeking out solitude: Robert de Tombelaine (a work on the Song of Songs) and Anastase le Vénitien, a renowned Hellenist and Latinist (1048).

In 1137 the reformer Bernard du Bec had a priory and three cells built as a retreat for the mount's monks, who were to go there in turn. The abbot added the chapel of Sainte-Marie-la-Gisante, the starting point of the pilgrimage dedicated to the Virgin, complementary to that of Saint Michael. Processions setting off from the mount sometimes made a detour by Tombelaine.

The 13th century saw fortifications by Philippe-Auguste, then—provoked by the monks— the exile of Jourdain, the worldly abbot behind the construction of the Merveille, with its ceremonial space, the Salle des Hôtes.

The years 1356–80 saw the first occupation by the English (of the Hundred Years War), who were to return from around 1420 to 1450.

The English fortified the islet, equipping it with a garrison. The mount withstood the siege and never surrendered.

During a truce, around 1420, "the River Couesnon in its madness" decided one fine morning to move north, between the mount and Tombelaine. It provided a sporadic extra moat for the mount and a natural defence for Tombelaine, once again English. But above all, it was yet another handicap for the enemy. The English, already forced to deal with the traps posed by the *tangue* (quicksand) and the ebb tide, henceforth had to cross the Couesnon with heavy siege engines, including the bombards that may still be seen behind the Porte de l'Avancée.

In 1420 Abbot Jolivet, who was to defect to the English, had 3,000 pounds of lead taken from the chapel of Saint-Antoine for a cistern on the mount. The pilgrims stopping off at Tombelaine had to pay a toll to the English to continue their journey to Mont-Saint-Michel: the enemy took the opportunity to search to see if they were transporting arms for the mount's defence. Antiterrorism measures were already in place…

It is said that in the 16th century, the Protestants of Montgomery's troop discreetly melted down sacred objets d'art on the islet stolen from churches to counterfeit coins.

In 1666 Louis XIV hounded his former finance minister to the very bay. Nicolas Fouquet had acquired Tombelaine. Fouquet had apparently chosen Tombelaine as bastion of rebellion against the king. Louis XIV, upon discovering the plan, was said to have decided to raze all Tombelaine's buildings. This was carried out by the marquis who governed the mount at the time. At court, some laid it on thick, saying that the English could come back and use the islet as their base.

Around 1925, with the beginning of the fashion for suntans, Tombelaine attracted investors. In their eyes, including those of a Monuments Historiques architect, the arid rock could become a seaside resort to rival the Riviera. A company was thus set up, the Groupement National de la Baie du Mont-Saint-Michel, which elaborated a grandiose project with villas, hotel, and casino. Some had faith in it, but all their fine money was lost in a resounding failure. The French state bought Tombelaine in 1933.

An odd character, the "Marquis de Tombelaine", should not go without mention. Around 1875 Jean Gauthier, a vagabond, moved into a hut on the islet. He guided the teams of animals and "holidaymakers" crossing the shore. The "marquis" had long hair and a prophet's beard, lived on tips, and was a hale and hearty habitué of the bistros of the mount and beyond. In the end, it was water that was his undoing. In 1892, on a day that he was drunk, the connoisseur of the bay's traps drowned in the flood tide. The Marquis de Tombelaine had another nickname: Jean le Déluge (John Flood).

Robert de Torigni, king of the abbots, abbot of the kings

Between 1100 and 1150, collapsing buildings, fires, and increasingly frequent quarrels with the dukes of Normandy meant that the order was in bad shape. The abbey was not doing well and neither were its finances. In 1154 Abbot Robert de Torigni was appointed by his royal protector, Henry II Plantagenet, king of England and duke of Normandy (who visited the mount three times). A skilful courtier and diplomat, the abbot engineered the reconciliation of Louis VII and Henry II, the new husband of Eleanor of Aquitaine, recently repudiated by the king of France. A man heeded by two popes—an arriviste according to his detractors—he got the cult of Saint Michael back on its feet again and recruited prolifically. The number of monks rose to sixty. His efficient management helped sort out the weakened abbey's finances. He behaved like a real temporal lord. He enlarged the abbey's fief, which at the time comprised dozens of bishoprics, parishes, priories, villages, ports, fisheries, mills, forests, saltworks, vineyards, various concerns, cattle farms, and hunting grounds, with rights, of course. The mount was never again as powerful; its influence extended from Cornwall to the Loire estuary via the islands near the River Cotentin. Torigni was a builder. To welcome high-ranking pilgrims, he had a three-storey hostelry (which collapsed in 1818) built on the south-west side of the rock. On the west slope, he treated himself to a building, now below the church square terrace. Under his apartments, he had two dungeons built—in addition to his rank as bishop, he assumed the privileges of justice. Near the dungeons, another room housed one of the *fillettes*, the sinister and barbaric cages prized by Louis XI. Torigni added two towers to the abbey church's façade. The tower on the left collapsed in 1300, leading to the destruction of hundreds of works in the rich library set up by the abbot. The mount was then known as the "City of Books", such was the reputation of its manuscripts in Europe. It was the zenith of the mount's spiritual renown. Torigni, a practitioner of fine literature, made the most of the in-house talents of the scriptorium and collected hundreds of texts produced at the mount, as well as from elsewhere. These documents concerned the sacred, the liturgy, the teachings of the Fathers of the Church, as well as the secular world: history, science, astronomy, mathematics, geometry, the ancient thinkers, etc.

As a historian, the abbot gave an account of the current events of his era in a chronicle. He encouraged a young monk from his "team", Guillaume de Saint Pair, to write a long poem in Vulgar Latin, recounting the saga of the mount. From 1154 to 1186 there were thirty-two years of abbacy and prosperity, of course, but there was one regret: Torigni, a major figure amongst the fifty-one abbots, did not take advantage of the Gothic impetus. He could have been the one to launch the building of the Merveille.

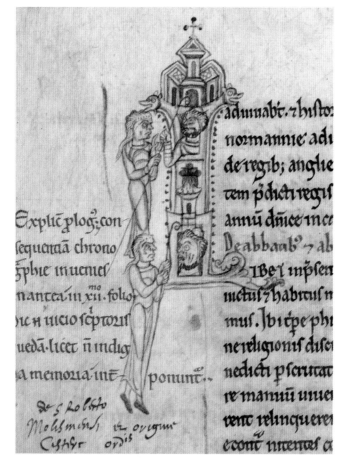

Decorated initial L of "*liber*". *Chronique historique de l'abbé Robert de Torigni*, 12th century. The two long-haired figures are perhaps the dukes of Normandy who hold out a bishop's crosier to two monks.
The top monk accepts it; the monk on the bottom refuses it. This was an allusion to the suzerains who wanted to choose the abbot, while the community sought to elect him from amongst its monks (Avranches, Bibliothèque Municipale, ms. 159, fol. 170 verso).

The other side of the magical picture

In 1863, despite petitions and tearful letters from inhabitants of the mount making a living from the prison, Napoleon III closed it. In the end, the living conditions of the mount's prisoners had aroused the indignation of the whole country. In its squalid jails, 14,000 people did time, some of them dying behind bars, from the French Revolution to 1863, over a period of only about seventy years. In 1836 Victor Hugo, with his companion Juliette Drouet, visited the veritable labyrinth. Hugo, once again, did not mince words: "It is all the noise of bolts, the noise of looms, shadows guarding shadows working, ghosts in rags moving in the pallid light . . . the admirable Salle des Chevaliers, now a workshop in which one watches hideous and grey men who look like enormous spiders bustle about through a skylight."

It did not escape the notice of kings, the French Republic, and emperors that the Norman islet, encircled by sand and waves, was the ideal location for a branch of the Bastille prison; it later replaced the Bastille after the Parisian fortress was razed to the ground. The black legend of the mount's prison, from which no one, or very few, escaped, began with the dungeons installed in the four corners of the abbey, whose *vade in pace* (go in peace) oubliettes were installed for monks who were delinquent or did not respect their vows. The imprisoned were sometimes briefly forgotten, but some of them died in their dungeons. The Hundred Years War saw the incarceration of many English soldiers, who were only freed after the payment of a large ransom. In the 12th century, Abbot Robert de Torigni, who acted like a baron and prefect, had merciless twin prison cells put in underneath his new residence. Around 1260, another authoritarian abbot had the Belle-Chaise built near the new east entrance. It was the local law court, which supplied the dungeons and even the gallows standing near the village gate with occupants.

The real "vocation" of the "Bastille by the sea" began during the reign of Louis XI. The pious king, and devotee of Saint Michael, discovered during his pilgrimages all the advantages of the strategically located islet in the shape of a small, chiselled mountain. So, in 1472, he sent one of his savage *fillettes* there. Louis XI, the Universal Spider, could thus ensnare the disgraced persons who burdened him—faraway. A *fillette* was a narrow cage of wooden bars reinforced with metal, and hung from the ceiling of a cellar near the twin prison cells. It was a form of torture of unnameable cruelty.

Noël Béda, an academic who dared to poke fun at the Field of the Cloth of Gold meeting between François I and Henry VIII of England, sampled the *fillette* for two years, dying in it. A Maurist Benedictine who published a *Le Cochon mitré* (The Mitred Pig), a lampoon of the archbishop of Reims, who was none other than the brother of Louvois (Louis XIV's secretary of state), rotted in the cage for twenty years, eventually losing his mind. In 1746 Victor de La Cassagne, known as Dubourg, spent 368 days in the diabolical cage before going mad and letting himself die of hunger. The poor wretch had only lampooned Louis XV, known as the Well-Beloved. In 1785 the vile cage was still in use; its (last?) occupant, the Chevalier d'Evelimont, accused of embezzlement, was caged up for nine days.

During the *Ancien Régime*, the mount's prisoners were there by order of the king, upon the delivery of a *lettre de cachet*, *petit* or *grand*: 153 from 1666 to 1789. The *petits cachets*, which made up the majority, were interned on demand or denunciation by their closest relatives because they were spendthrifts, violent, on the margins of society, or debauched, like Stapleton, of Irish origin, who stewed in prison for twenty-four years. The *grands exilés* were sent to the mount by royal arbitrary power. The grounds? Political, conspiracy, fraud, dubious financial dealings, fraudulent bankruptcy, and debt, not forgetting the great number of priests and monks, the Maurists of Mont-Saint-Michel included, guilty of Jansenism. The king's prisoners, watched over by the jailer in chef, the abbey prior, were judged for the most part in the abbatial residences. A few of the more privileged ones were half-free, like the

Comte d'Esparbès, who lived with his family and moved freely on the mount. Therefore, *lettres de cachet* did not always end in imprisonment.

Louis XIV abused his kingly power. Thus, the Armenian patriarch Avedick, having made unkind remarks about the Sun King, found himself in the shadow of the abbey for some years, after having been abducted on the Aegean island of Chios. As for the iron mask, caught sight of everywhere, it was also pure fabrication.

Les Fanils at the bottom of the mount's south slope. Built in 1828, this barracks housed about a hundred prison guards, who watched over several hundreds of men, women, and children. The building succeeded the abbey's former warehouses.

This "funicular" with wooden rails, is the dray ladder on the south side. The nearly vertical stone ladder, installed by the prison management in around 1818, allowed the abbey, transformed into a prison, to be resupplied.

Late 19th century: the north transept of the church seen from the cloister, where the garden had not yet been laid out. Clearly, restoration was imperative as its being used as an extension of the prison did a lot of damage to the abbey, as did the twelfth fire in 1834 (Paris, MAP).

A nightmarish heap

The French Revolution drove out the last monks and set a few prisoners free. And yet the sans-culottes saved the "Bastille by the sea", not razing it, quite the opposite. The former Mont-Michel became Mont-Libre (ironically "Free Mount"), a prison—and nothing more. The first internees were the hundreds of priests who had rejected the Civil Constitution of the Clergy. Then came the Chouans, and later the common-law criminals.

The year 1793 saw the imprisonment of the first "communist", conspirator Gracchus Babeuf. He was succeeded by member of the Convention (the assembly that governed France from 1792–95) Jean-Baptiste Lecarpentier, nicknamed the Bourreau de la Manche (Executioner of the Manche *Département*), imprisoned during the Restoration for having voted for the death of Louis XVI. The strangest thing was that the regicide's cellmate was the clog-maker Mathurin Bruneau, one of the thirty false dauphins claiming to be Louis XVII. One wanted to kill the king; the other said he was his son.

In 1811 Napoleon decreed the mount a prison, more or less for his opponents. Louis XVIII did one better, transforming the establishment into a prison and reformatory for men and women condemned to hard labour. The arrival of old convicts and those waiting to be deported completed the idyllic scene. The mount had up to 800 inmates at a time, including 80 children less than 16 years of age. To provide them with supplies, around 1820 the prison administration installed a "dray ladder" in the former monks' ossuary on the south side of the rock. As during the Middle Ages, for the Romanesque store-room, then that of the Merveille (from which Protestants made a failed attempt to invade the mount in the 16th century), it was a kind of steeple-jack crane, a large wooden "drum" wheel 6 metres in diameter, powered by several prisoners marching inside. This dray ladder, including the wheel and the slide, may still be seen at the entrance of the opening made in the former monks' ossuary. It could haul up the "wagon" containing 2 tonnes of provisions on a nearly vertical stone ramp installed on the slope of the mount. All the abbey's rooms were mobilised at the time, defaced by their prison functions. Even the cloister was used as a gymnasium! The Salle des Chevaliers was a spinning and weaving workshop (which Victor Hugo wrote about) for men; the refectory, adapted on three levels, was used as an embroidery workshop and dormitory for women. The women also sewed sailcloth in the Salle des Hôtes, whose guards turned them out so that they could sleep. Felt was worked in the ambulatory, later used to store wood. Except for the choir, which was cut off by a curtain, the abbey church was divided into two levels: the upper floor as a dormitory and the ground floor as a refectory and workshop for straw hats, shoes, and clogs. Such crowding meant that disease, including typhoid fever, mange, and tuberculosis, wreaked havoc. There were 457 deaths between 1820 and 1830 alone.

In 1832 the "political prisoners" landed. There were seventy-seven of them, mainly Vendean royalists, legitimists, republicans, and democrats (including the painter Édouard Colombat, one of the very few who managed to escape from Mont-Saint-Michel).

In 1839 the unshakeable and unruly "reds" arrived, such as Armand Barbès, "the rebel", and Louis Auguste Blanqui, "the locked-up one", eternal conspirators perpetually contemplating escape. As they failed to do so, these two rebels were sentenced to five months of solitary confinement in the *loges* (1.6 by 2 metre dungeons) built above the cloister galleries. Demolished in 1860, these appalling dungeons recalled the horrendous Piombi prisons of Venice. There was another lugubrious echo: the *loges*, practically cloned from the cages de Louis XI, were the *fillettes* of the reign of Louis-Philippe. When he visited the mount, the future king, still young, ordered the *fillette*, "monument of barbarity", to be destroyed.

In 1863 there was widespread protest against the conditions of incarceration on the mount. Bowing to public opinion, and that of deputies, Napoleon III closed the prison: a catastrophe for the mount's inhabitants. In 1850 there were still 1,182 of them, convicts included. In 1866 the population of the village fell to 203 inhabitants. However, the end of the prison prosperity was also the beginning of the mount's second life. Pilgrimages began again around 1860–65, increasing in number from 1870–71, with the support of the "clerical party". And above all, this period marked the beginning of the influx of tourists—aided by the railways followed by automobiles and sped up by the restoration of the buildings—the redemption of the prison mount.

Pilgrimage fever, famous relics

The rite of pilgrimage dates back to the ancient Orient (the Three Wise Men). The clerics of the Early Middle Ages did not need to preach because the call of God and Saint Michael was so urgent. One had to unburden one's soul at the mount and be listened to by the archangel in order to be accompanied to Heaven by him. Saint Michael pilgrimages spread all over Europe, especially in the 14th century, a gloomy era: wars, plague, poverty, the fear of hell (dances of death). Ten or so "paths to the mount" attracted pious travellers from all over. It was the journey of their lives. Wrapped in their capes, the pilgrims—*miquelots*—travelled 30 kilometres a day. They were sometimes accommodated in hospices, the *sauvetées*. In 1368, 16,690 pilgrims visited the abbey. There they found the aid of the monks: board and lodging, bandages, prayers, and relics. This was undoubtedly Heaven's antechamber. This fever even mobilised children. In 1333, *pastoureaux*, young shepherds, flooded in from all over western France. In 1457, just after the Hundred Years War, the youthful devoutness resumed with 4,000 adolescents from Flanders, Languedoc, Switzerland, Germany, Poland, etc. Crosses sewn on to the fronts and backs of their garments, these youngsters made a crusade without conquests. The Earthly Jerusalem was no longer accessible, so the mount—the Heavenly Jerusalem—was chosen for the wild adventure of pilgrimage.

Little inclined to risk their necks on the dangerous roads, those of high rank delegated to replacements, vicarious pilgrims.

This human tide was raised by the impulses of the soul. The impetus was that of the desire to make contact with the archangel: a palpable revelation of the invisible. However, this influx of faith travellers was also due in part to the universal fame of the relics, beginning with the mount's key piece, the rock itself. Especially since the abbots deliberately left it visible here and there, in the Grand Degré Intérieur (Great Inner Staircase) or in some of the abbey's sanctuaries. The number of relics multiplied; they were all certified as genuine by the monks, who added to their renown by increasing the number of accounts of local miracles. One example was the story of the stone with the name of Jesus in Latin carved onto it that fell directly on the mount in the 13th century. Kings brought their own donations, like Philippe le Bel with two thorns from the Crown of Thorns and a fragment of the True Cross. In the 12th century, forty-nine relics were venerated in Notre-Dame-sous-Terre and especially in the south transept of the abbey church. In the 18th century, the collection was at its maximum, 246 relics representing about 150 saints. To cure his earthly ills miraculously, the pilgrim went to touch the relics or rub himself with water in which the preferred relic had been steeped. In the Middle Ages, they really believed in the power of relics, just as we trust in science in the 21st century. On the mount, the display case of house relics was diversified and included the pierced skull (which may still be viewed in the church of Saint-Gervais d'Avranches) said to belong to Bishop Aubert, founder of the cult of Saint Michael. The "print" of the archangel's finger was thought to be only that of a cyst, a benign tumour that did not kill the cleric, who lived with a big bump on the right side of his head. There is also one of the same Aubert's arms, Saint John the Baptist's tooth, Saint Vincent's finger, Saint Benedict's blood (?), a coal (?) from Saint Lawrence's grill, a bit of Christ's crib (?), a few threads from the Virgin's veil, along with a few of her hairs, thorns from the Crown of Thorns, shards of the (True) Cross, a fragment of the Holy Sponge (without the vinegar), a piece of the handkerchief (?) used to mop Christ's forehead, and, most plausibly, a few tufts of Saint Francis's hair (he was a contemporary of the Merveille as he was canonised in 1228).

The powers attributed to the relics included just about everything, with a few specialities: blindness, deafness, barrenness, persistent migraine (Aubert), stiff neck (?), palsy, demonic possession, etc. Calvin delighted in poking fun at the 6,666 pieces of the skull of Saint John the Baptist.

These relics were honoured with long, slow, solemn processions, with chants, psalms, and incantations during the stations marking out the route, particularly on the landings of the Grand Degré stairs. These were ceremonies of humility to ask Saint Michael if one could go directly to paradise without spending time in purgatory first.

Relieved and full of hope, the pilgrims wanted to bring back evidence of their presence on the mount. Tearing off a piece of the rock was not easy, and forbidden. So they gathered shells from the bay. From the 13th century, the archangel's yes-men fell upon the stalls selling mass-produced pious souvenirs. The village, inhabited by a few fishermen at the time, soon realised that the trade of the merchants of the temple

The Dream of Saint Aubert, cartulary of Mont-Saint-Michel, *c.* 1150 (152 pages bound in the 17th century). A legend embellished with gold dust: accompanied by more or less harmonious music, Saint Michael points an authoritarian index finger at the head of Bishop Aubert, demanding a sanctuary dedicated to him at the top of the mount. The sanctuary is depicted in the image as a building that was half church, half fortress (Avranches, Bibliothèque Municipale, ms. 210, fol. 4 verso).

V'AINS, En pèlerinage au Mont Saint-Michel

In the early 20th century, the rite of Saint Michael became a regular occurrence once again: this procession makes its way along the causeway, built in 1879.
To the left, the rails of the steam tram installed in 1901.

was profitable. The innkeepers were not all honest. Some were swindlers who duped the naive pilgrims. Even worse were the shore guides who did not hesitate to lose their clients in the fog and the dangers of the bay. Distinguished pilgrims brought back gold or silver medals. The modest ones contented themselves with the certificates of passage,

religious trinkets, and badges sold by the *biblotiers*: lead or tin flasks filled with sand from the bay or wax drippings from the altar candles. On the return journey, the pilgrims met admirers paying their share to touch the pious souvenirs. During the Renaissance, the great humanist Erasmus poked fun at this credulous consumption of "hardware".

139 LE MONT SAINT-MICHEL. — *Voiture de Genêts traversant la Grève.* - LL.

In the early 20th century, whether pilgrims or the first tourists, the mount's visitors really liked to use the *maringuottes*. These horse-drawn carts allowed them to cross nearly 6 kilometres of strand, from Genêts on the Cotentin coast.

Mont-Saint-Michel at risk from the land

Sand sounding the retreat is no longer an old dream. The mount will finally become an island once again, slowly but surely. It will no longer look like a granite ship run aground in France's largest bay of its type with several estuaries: 40,000 hectares. Soon the mount will again have its feet in the water, at least 150 days of "spring tides" a year, compared with 35–55 on average for many decades. In the Middle Ages, seafarers sailed around the mount. Thus in 1425, in the middle of the Hundred Years War, sailors from Saint-Malo broke the blockade by English ships to provide the inhabitants of the mount with fresh supplies. But the invading sand never ended its blockade. The silting of the bay began as soon as the hillocks of the mount and Tombelaine became islands as a result of the floods resulting from the thaw of the last glaciation. From around 8000 BC, unflaggingly, tide after tide (100 million cubic metres of water twice daily), the sea comes out with it: a million more cubic metres of sand each year. More sediment arrives than departs since the low tide has one-third less energy than the high tide. As a result, the bay's silting is 7–14 metres thick in places.

The sand is *tangue* (a word of Viking origin), an argilo-calcareous conchiferous filler. From the 12th to the 19th century, it was widely used as a soil improver. However, the removal of 500,000 cubic metres annually was not enough to slow the silting. All the more so as man, since the 11th century,

has not stopped modifying the nature of the bay in various ways, thus speeding up the silting process. With the consent of the mount's abbots, real businessmen with an interest in the bay's prosperity and its various businesses, including the countless small-scale saltworks, the mud flats were transformed into salt marshes. These native pastures proved excellent for the rearing of thousands of salt meadow sheep, which grazed on grass covered from time to time by the spring tides. After several attempts, notably in 1838, dykes were put up during the Second Empire to polderise the salt marshes. It was the beginning of the remarkably fertile agricultural polders for market gardening (carrots). After having eaten away at the bay for a century, the surface area of the polders has been fixed since 1933, but they only ended a kilometre from the mount. As for the salt marshes, through the continuous addition of mud and *tangue*, they did not stop encircling the mount: 20 to 40 additional hectares some years. The 19th century made the situation worse by changing the terminal course, the estuary of the three coastal rivers: the Sée, the Sélune, and especially the Couesnon, with its irregular rate of flow and capricious shifting. Let us recall the famous expression of centuries past: "The Couesnon in its madness put the mount in Normandy." The saying conveys the bitterness of Bretons annoyed at seeing the mount annexed by their neighbours. The inconstant Couesnon, changing its bed as the mood took it, has been channelled since 1863, then constrained in 1969 with an outflow dam. The natural flushing out of sediments by the coastal rivers was impeded by these hydraulic modifications. One of the most regrettable improvements was none other than the 2-kilometre causeway erected in 1879 between the mainland and the mount. The Ponts and Chaussées (the engineer Dinet) stupidly had it put up between two rampart towers and not at the village gate, the Porte de l'Avancée. The causeway is a regrettable barrier that blocks the currents, leading to an accumulation of *tangue* on either side. In short, a series of errors that the sand-removal works will, for the most part, remedy. Operations began in 2006, thanks to the mixed private-public partnership, grouping together the principal local authorities, to the make the mount an island once more. The Heavenly Jerusalem's restored independence will cost around 200 million euros, the

equivalent of 25 kilometres of motorway. The mount is worth it.

Although long and difficult to implement, the works aim to clear a large part of the sediments left by the low tide. To do this, the new dam on the estuary of the Couesnon, with 8 floodgates and 2 fish locks, lets the sea water enter, stocking some 1.5 million cubic metres, including the flow of the Couesnon. Then, accompanying the ebb tide, the dam "flushes", without breaking waves, to sweep a maximum amount of sediment out to sea. The essential complement of this unique equipment is the removal, eventually, of the harmful causeway. There are plans to replace it with a 2.2-kilometre way with three sections starting at the place known as the Caserne: 1,200 metres of causeway on the salt marshes, then 800 metres of footbridge over the restored currents, then 200 metres of submersible platform ending at the Porte de l'Avancée. The two hideous car parks at the foot of the mount (up to 10,000 vehicles a day in July and August) will be replaced by 4,140 new parking spots at the mainland entrance of the new way. Visitors will be transported by a frequent, and silent, shuttle service. The idea behind the new umbilical cord between the mainland and the mount is also that of a moment of real wonder for pedestrians. As a result of the gravitational force of the sluicing, the water should go back to its old ways. The effect of the flushing out should be noticeable by 2015

or 2020, and things should be much better beginning in 2025.

In 1879, after the opening of the causeway, the newspaper *La France* was already worried about the bay getting rapidly "stuck in the sand". Around the same time, Victor Hugo, a mount regular who militated in its favour, protested about the new peninsula: "Mont-Saint-Michel is to France what the Great Pyramid is to Egypt. It must be saved from mutilation. The mount must remain an island. This double masterpiece of nature and art must be preserved at all costs." The disaster of the nearly filled-in bay threatened: in 1894 it was planned that the polders would come up to the mount. Even worse, in the 17th century, Vauban, while inspecting the mount, was disappointed by the fortified enclosure, which was ineffectual to deal with new advances in artillery, and turned his attention to the site. He advised the Sun King to divert the rivers Sée, Sélune, and Couesnon towards the Rance Basin and transform the bay into a meadow. There is no doubt that without measures against its silting up, in a few centuries the bay will be nothing but green countryside. The harnessed tide and the Couesnon are now allies in prolonging the mechanical effect of the ebb tide. This clearing of the layer of *tangue* should create a new landscape around Mont-Saint-Michel. Guided by the new configuration of the sand, reinforced by the flushing action

of the sea, the Couesnon may well separate into two branches, one to the north between Tombelaine and the mount, the other to the south. That is, a River Couesnon that is both Norman and Breton.

Such is the strange uncertainty of sand and water.

In his 1906 guide, one of the best architects and restorers of the mount, Paul Gout, denounced the accelerated polderisation of the bay, "which will have largely lost its prestigious character when its ring of ramparts emerges from salt marshes or potato fields".

In 1879 the conflict between the architect and restorer Édouard Corroyer and the Ponts et Chaussées engineer resulted in the aberration of the causeway ending between the Tour du Roi to the left and the Tour de l'Arcade to the right.

Centre des monuments nationaux

President
Isabelle Lemesle
General director
Fabrice Benkimoun

Éditions du patrimoine

Publishing director
Jocelyn Bouraly
Publications coordinator
Clair Morizet
Assistant publications coordinator
Karin Franques
Editorial and documentation coordinator
Anne-Sophie Grouhel-Le Tellec

Graphic design
Cyril Cohen
Régis Dutreuil

Production coordinator
Carine Merse

Translator
Chrisoula Petridis

Copy editor
Susan Schneider

Photoengraving
APS-Chromostyle, Tours

Printing
Mame, Tours, France
Dépôt légal: November 2008

Reprinting
IME, Baume-les-Dames, France
June 2011

© Éditions du patrimonine
Centre des monuments nationaux
Paris, 2008
ISBN: 978-2-7577-0014-3
ISSN: 1960-3304

Acknowledgements

The author would like to thank warmly
the director of Mont-Saint-Michel for the kindly interest
he has shown in this project.

Photographic credits

Yann Arthus-Bertrand/Altitude: 61
Avranches, Bibliothèque Municipale: 6, 59, 60, 62, 65
Philippe Body/Hoa-Qui/Eyedea: 22
Hervé Champollion/akg-images: 29r, 31r, 34t
CMN/Philippe Berthé: 2–3, 13r, 16l, 21r, 23, 38, 40l, 42r, 44, 45,
48, 49l, 51, 52–53, 56–57, 66, 67
CMN/Patrick Cadet: 7, 13l, 14, 15
CMN/Daniel Chenot: 12, 16r, 25r, 28–29, 32–33, 36, 37, 39, 40r,
41, 42l, 43, 46, 47, 49r, 50, 54, 63
CMN/Médiathèque de l'Architecture et du Patrimoine,
Archives Photos/reproduction Philippe Berthé: 4, 13c, 64
CMN/Marc Rapilliard: 17, 18, 19, 20-21, 24–25, 26, 27, 30–31
CMN/Étienne Revault: 35
CMN/T. Valès: 34b
A. Kubacsi/Explorer/Eyedea: 58
Logis Tiphaine: 10
Bildarchiv Monheim/akg-images: 55
Steve Vidler/Imagestate/GHFP/Eyedea: front cover

Illustrations, cover, and opening pages

Front cover: South façade of Mont-Saint-Michel.
Page 17: With the patience of an angel, Saint Michael has been
on watch from the top of his 157-metre pedestal since 1897.
The idea for this statue came from Victor Petitgrand: the architect
and restorer claimed that there had already been a gilt statue
of Saint Michael at the top of the bell tower in the late 16th century.
Wearing a copper pourpoint adorned with gold leaf, 4.5 metres tall,
and weighing nearly half a tonne, Saint Michael, whose wings
and sword end in lightning rods, defies the thunderbolts.
Page 58: Pilgrims crossing the Bay of Mont-Saint-Michel.

Abbreviations

AP: Archives Photographiques
CMN: Centre des Monuments Nationaux
MAP: Médiathèque de l'Architecture and du Patrimoine